PUPPET SKITS

David C Cook
transforming lives together

Cool Puppet Skits for the Park Patrol to Perform

NOAH'S PARK® CHILDREN'S CHURCH PUPPET SKITS (Green Edition)
Published by David C. Cook
4050 Lee Vance View
Colorado Springs, CO 80918 U.S.A.

David C. Cook Distribution Canada
55 Woodslee Avenue Paris, Ontario, Canada N3L 3E5

David C. Cook U.K., Kingsway Communications
Eastbourne, East Sussex BN23 6NT, England

David C. Cook and the graphic circle C logo are registered trademarks of Cook
Communications Ministries.

Product Developer:	Karen Pickering
Managing Editor:	Doug Schmidt
Editor:	Judy Gillispie
Contributing Writers:	René Stewart, Diane Cory, Nancy Sutton, Karen Schmidt, Gail Rohlfing
Interior Design:	Mike Riester
Cover Design:	Todd Mock
Illustrations:	Aline Heiser, Chris Sharp

All Scripture quotations, unless otherwise stated, are from the Holy Bible, New
International Version®, NIV®. Copyright © 1973, 1978, 1984 by Biblica, Inc.™
Used by permission of Zondervan. All rights reserved worldwide.
www.zondervan.com

ISBN 978-0-7814-3845-2

First Printing 2002
Printed in the United States

5 6 7 8 9 10 11 12 13 14

100610

TABLE OF CONTENTS

INTRODUCTION

Puppets can be a great addition to a children's ministry program. Through the use of puppets Bible truths can be reinforced and the children can gain a better understanding of how to apply these Bible truths to their own lives.

Two puppets are included in this Children's Church Kit. The puppet personalities are listed on GP·5 of this book. After you identify your puppets and understand their personalities, it can help as you or the Park Patrol members present the puppet skits. (If you would like to purchase additional puppets to use in your program, call 1-800-323-7543 or visit our Web site at www.DavidCCook.com.)

There is one puppet skit provided to correlate with each week's Bible story. For the puppet skit presentation, we suggest that you combine the Elementary and Preschool children. If you have an exceptionally large Children's Church and would like to keep the Elementary and Preschoolers separated for the entire program, you might want to consider having more than one puppet theater and purchasing additional puppets.

You will want to train the Park Patrol members by using the Park Patrol Training Book. This training will help them confidently use the puppets and present the skits.

Have fun as you use these puppets and skits. Remember that this is a ministry that can have a great impact on your students!

PERSONALITIES

PONDER the Frog

Ponder the frog is the leader that everyone looks up to in Noah's Park. He watched Noah and Noah's relationship with God and now tries to help the other animals understand how God can help them in their everyday lives. Favorite quote: "I remember the ark!"

HONK the Camel

Honk the purple camel hates dirt; he loves to be clean. Honk is proud of his looks, from his clean and shiny fur to the proud gleam in his eye. Favorite quote: "I'm one good-looking camel."

DREAMER the Rhinoceros

Dreamer the blue rhinoceros is a very sweet and very sleepy animal. Dreamer loves to sleep, loves to dream, and loves to dream about sleeping. Favorite quote: "When I dream, I can do anything!"

STRETCH the Giraffe

Stretch the giraffe is the big sister to all the animals in Noah's Park. She is kind, generous, and very naive. Favorite quote: "I am curious about everything!"

STRETCH

PONDER

DREAMER

HONK

PUPPET THEATRES

Set up your puppet theater in a place apart from the Bible story area or the snacks, games, and crafts areas. That way the Park Patrol members can be setting up and be prepared to perform the day's puppet skit just as soon as you move the children to the puppet skit location. It will also make it obvious to the children that this is a special part of the program.

The following suggestions are given for some simple puppet theaters. Decide on the type of puppet theater by considering the space you have available and the cost of preparation. Be sure to have the puppet theater constructed before working with the Park Patrol for training. They will need to actually use the puppet theater, puppets, and skits as they practice to become proficient for this part of your program.

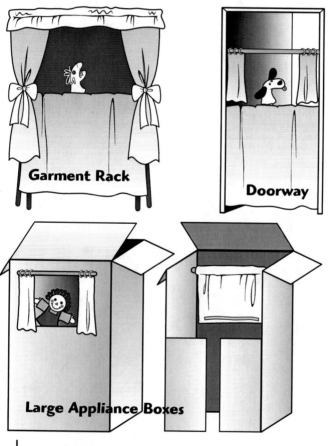

Garment Rack

Doorway

Large Appliance Boxes

GP1: Spinfitzle

Cast: Noah's Park Puppet, adult leader

Puppet hurries onstage to the leader.

NP PUPPET: *Is that what I think it is? (Points back offstage.)*

LEADER: *That depends. What are you talking about, and what do you think something is?*

NP PUPPET: *I think that purple, orange, and green food backstage is Spinfitzle.*

LEADER: *You'd be right. It's grape-flavored custard with orange marmalade and a pickle.*

NP PUPPET: *I knew it! I knew it! Spinfitzle is my favorite food. Do I get to eat it?*

LEADER: *You could . . .*

NP PUPPET: *Great! This is a great day!*

LEADER: *But I wouldn't if I were you.*

NP PUPPET: *Why not?*

LEADER: *Because you get a tummy ache every time you eat Spinfitzle.*

NP PUPPET: *Do not.*

LEADER: *Do too.*

NP PUPPET: *Do not. You just don't want me to eat my favorite food in the whole world.*

LEADER: *I don't care if you eat it, but if you eat it, you'll get a tummy ache.*

NP PUPPET: *I will not. And . . . I can prove it. I saw that Spinfitzle, and I already ate it. (Speaks to the kids.)* **Do you want any, kids?** *(Listens to responses and nods.)*

LEADER: **Well,** *(Name of puppet.),* **I guess I was . . .** *(Puppet moans and holds stomach.)* **I was . . .** *(Puppet moans.)* **What's wrong?**

NP PUPPET: **My tummy hurts.** *(Moans.)* **How did you know I'd get a tummy ache?**

LEADER: **Oh,** *(Name of puppet.),* **sit down. Do you know how Jesus knows ALL about you? Well, sometimes adults know a lot about you too. You're important to me.**

NP PUPPET: *I wish I had listened to you. I feel like I'm going to throw . . . (Runs off stage.)*

GP2: A Heavy Load

Cast: Ponder the Frog Puppet

Props: Large Bible

PONDER: *(Standing by a Bible.)* **Hi, kids. I'm Ponder. How are you?** *(Wait for kids' answer.)* **I'm not doing so well today. I've got a big problem. Do you see this Bible?** *(Noah's Park Puppet points to Bible in front of it and waits for children to answer.)*

It's just too heavy. I wish *(Name of the leader.)* **were here. She would be able to lift it for me. I've tried and tried, but I still can't lift it. I drank milk so that my bones would be strong.** *(Strikes a pose that shows he is strong.)* **But I guess my bones aren't strong enough.**

I exercise regularly. *(Runs back and forth across the stage to show exercising.)* **And still I find that there are some things that I just can't do.** *(Tries again to pick up the Bible but can't.)*

Hmmm. I wonder . . . *(Looks back and forth between the kids and at the Bible.)* **I don't think** *(Name of one outgoing child.)* **is getting my hint. What should I do? Should I ask for help? That's it!**

(Turns to child named.) **Excuse me,**

(Name of child.). **Would you be able to pick up this Bible for me and move it to the shelf?**

(If child says, "No," then the puppet says, **"It's too hard for me, too,"** *and asks another child to put it on the shelf.)*

Thank you so much, *(Name of child who helped.).* **You're a lot like Jesus. He helps us when we ask, just as you helped me. We're that important to Him.**

(Pause as if thinking.) **Oh, wow! I just thought of something. I must be important to you, too! Yippee!** *(Runs off stage excitedly.)* **Yeah! Yahoo! Yippee! I'm important to** *(Name of child who helped.)***!**

Lesson G2: Ask Jesus | GP•10

GP3: A Scientific Belief

Cast: Noah's Park Puppet, a Leader

Leader walks by Noah's Park Puppet.

NP PUPPET: *(Dramatically.)* **I believe in Jesus.** *(Pause. The next line should be said in a sing-song voice.)* **I believe in Jesus.** *(Pause. The next line should be said in a low, slow, deep voice)* **I believe in Jesus.**

LEADER: **What are you doing,** *(Name of puppet.)***?**

NP PUPPET: **I'm growing in my faith.**

LEADER: **How are you doing that?**

NP PUPPET: **I came up with a great system. I say, "I believe in Jesus," so many times that every pore in my body and every hair on my head can't help but believe in Jesus.**

LEADER: **You're going to believe in Jesus more because you've convinced your pores and hair to believe?** *(Laughs.)*

NP PUPPET: **Do you know a better way?**

LEADER: **Absolutely.**

NP PUPPET: **What way is that? And don't be surprised if I laugh at what you say. My way is very scientific.**

LEADER: *(Name of puppet.)*, **you're so**

> important to Jesus that He'll help you believe.

NP PUPPET: *How do you know that?*

LEADER: *Well, I was just walking by and heard you talking.*

NP PUPPET: *That sounds more like an accident than a scientific conclusion.*

LEADER: *(Laughs.) You're so important to God that He sent me to show you how to draw closer to Him.*

NP PUPPET: *You can do that?*

LEADER: *Let's see. I have my Bible. Yes, I'm sure I can.*

NP PUPPET: *Then what are we waiting for? (Both leave together.)*

GP4: An Important Secret

Cast: Noah's Park Puppet, Leader

NP Puppet hangs its head as if depressed.

NP PUPPET: *(Without enthusiasm.)* **It's my birthday.**

LEADER: **Well, happy birthday!**

NP PUPPET: *(Sighs.)* **Thanks.**

LEADER: **Why are you so unhappy? Don't you have birthday plans?**

NP PUPPET: *(Sounding sad.)* **My parents sent out invitations to all my animal friends.**

LEADER: **You're going to have a big party?**

NP PUPPET: *(Sounding miserable.)* **With a large Noah's Ark cake, party hats, and ice cream.**

LEADER: **Wow! That sounds great. When does it start?**

NP PUPPET: **Now.**

LEADER: **What are you doing here?**

NP PUPPET: *(Hesitates, then bursts out.)* **Something horrible has happened. My parents are keeping secrets from me. All week they've stopped talking when I entered the room. I think that maybe they don't like me anymore.**

LEADER: **Of course, they like you. You are so**

important to them that they've been making secret plans to give you a day of birthday surprises.

NP PUPPET: *You think so?*

LEADER: *I know so, because God's the same way. He's preparing unbelievable blessings for you, but he's not giving all the details yet either.*

NP PUPPET: *But that could only mean one thing.*

LEADER: *What's that?*

NP PUPPET: *I'm late. (Yells.) Mom! Dad! Here I come. Wait for me. Happy birthday to me. Happy birthday to me. . . . (Exits still singing to itself.)*

GP5: Just Like Dad

Cast: Noah's Park Puppet, Leader

Leader stands by NP Puppet.

NP PUPPET:	*Toss me a volleyball.*
LEADER:	*No.*
NP PUPPET:	*Are you afraid I'll spike it so hard that you won't even see it pass you?*
LEADER:	*No, I can't pass you a volleyball because I don't have a volleyball.*
NP PUPPET:	*Oh.*
LEADER:	*Are you really that good at volleyball?*
NP PUPPET:	*I'm pretty good, but you should see my dad. He's a great volleyball player.*
LEADER:	*No kidding.*
NP PUPPET:	*Toss me a football if you're not too chicken.*
LEADER:	*I'm not too chicken.*
NP PUPPET:	*Then toss it, and I'll throw it so hard that you'll be scared to catch it.*
LEADER:	*I can't throw a football to you because I don't have a football.*
NP PUPPET:	*Oh. Did you know that my dad's a great football player?*

LEADER: *Your dad sounds like an athlete.*

NP PUPPET: *Do you know him?*

LEADER: *No, but I see him in you, just as we can see God the Father through Jesus.*

NP PUPPET: *Jesus shows us what God is like?*

LEADER: *That's right.*

NP PUPPET: *That's neat. (Puffs out chest.) My dad's real cool.*

LEADER: *And you're just like him.*

NP PUPPET: *Yeah, I'm cool too.*

GP6: Jesus Can Heal

Cast: Ponder, Noah's Park Puppet 2

Props: Paper flower

Puppet 2 is onstage alone.

PUPPET 2: *Boy, is Ponder going to be mad. Look at those flowers. The neighbor's dog trampled all over them.* (Looks at kids.) *When Ponder comes by, would you tell him what Rover did? Just say, "Rover trampled your flowers." Okay, let's practice. When I point to you, say, "Rover trampled your flowers."* (Points to kids and waits for them to say their line.) *That was really good, but you can do even better. Let's try it again.* (Points to kids and waits.) *Great. Uh, oh! Here comes Ponder.*

PONDER: *Hi,* (Name of Puppet 2.)*. What's new?*

PUPPET 2: *Well, uh . . .* (Points to kids and waits for them to say their line.)

PONDER: *Not my flowers!* (Puts hands to head and hurries offstage.)

PUPPET 2: *Boy, was Ponder upset! I'm so glad you were here to help me. I hate giving people bad news.*

PONDER: (Returns carrying a flower.) *I was able to save one. I'm going to put it in a* *glass of water.*

PUPPET 2: *Did all the others die?*

PONDER: *No, they're perennials. That means that they grow back year after year. They will be back even stronger next year.*

PUPPET 2: *Perennials are a lot like people.*

PONDER: *You're right. They keep coming back no matter how sick or hurt they are.*

PUPPET 2: *But some die.*

PONDER: *Like this one. But I'm going to put it in water to keep it alive. It can't live in the garden like it used to, but I can still enjoy it.*

PUPPET 2: *That's like what Jesus does, Ponder. Sometimes He healed people when He lived on earth.*

PONDER: *And sometimes He still does, (Name of Puppet 2.). When Jesus heals people, that's a way that He shows us what God is like.*

PUPPET 2: *Can I watch you put that in water?*

PONDER: *Sure. Follow me. (Both exit.)*

GP7: A Real Kind of Love

Cast: Ponder, Noah's Park Puppet 2

Props: Pencil, cup, nail file, cotton-tipped swabs

Ponder holds a pencil and speaks to the audience, with Puppet 2 nearby. Ponder looks around for a place to lay down the pencil.

PUPPET 2: *Let me hold that for you.*

PONDER: *Thanks,* (Name of Puppet 2.). *(Puppet 2 runs off with pencil and comes back with a cup.)* **Today we are going to learn about . . .**

PUPPET 2: *Would you like a drink of water?*

PONDER: *Um, yes, thanks, I would.* (Ponder pretends to drink and gives the cup back to Puppet 2, who runs offstage.) *What was I saying? Let me think. Oh yes, I remember.*

(Puppet 2 returns with a nail file, grabs Ponder's hand and begins rubbing his nails.)

PONDER: *Today we are going to learn about . . .* (Ponder looks at Puppet 2.) **What are you doing?**

PUPPET 2: *I'm filing your nails.*

PONDER: *I can see that. But why?*

PUPPET 2: *Because I love you.*

PONDER: *You love me so you're filing my nails?*

PUPPET 2: *Yep. My, my, this hand is going to need some work.*

PONDER: *(Pulls hand away from Puppet 2.)* **I don't understand.**

PUPPET 2: *A lot of people think that hugging and kissing and all that mushy stuff means you love someone.*

PONDER: *Like we see on television?*

PUPPET 2: *Right. But Jesus showed us God's love by becoming a servant to us.*

PONDER: *You're right. Jesus washed His disciples' feet to show us God's love.*

PUPPET 2: *Of course, I'm right. So I'm going to serve you in every way possible. (Puts down nail file and picks up a cotton-tipped swab.)* **Now if you'll bend down, I'll just clean out that waxy buildup in your ears.**

PONDER: *(Throws arms up in alarm.)* **I'm not sure that's quite what Jesus meant!** *(Runs offstage, being chased by Puppet 2.)*

GP8: A Loud Forgiveness

Cast: Leader, Noah's Park Puppet

Leader and puppet are onstage.

NP PUPPET: *I forgive you.*

LEADER: *You forgive me?*

NP PUPPET: *Yes, I forgive you.*

LEADER: *But . . . I didn't do anything wrong.*

NP PUPPET: *(Yelling.)* *I'm trying to act like Jesus and show you how God forgives us when we're wrong. So . . . (In a soft, sweet voice.) I forgive you.*

LEADER: *(Looks amazed.)* *You can't forgive me if I haven't done anything wrong.*

NP PUPPET: *Can too.*

LEADER: *Cannot!*

NP PUPPET: *Can too.*

LEADER: *Cannot! What did I do? (Yells.) Tell me what I did!*

NP PUPPET: *You just yelled at me.*

LEADER: *But, but . . .*

NP PUPPET: *You don't have to apologize.*

LEADER: *But I'm not . . .*

NP PUPPET: *It's okay.*

LEADER: *But you . . .*

NP PUPPET: *You see, God forgives us when we do wrong. So I know just what Jesus would do.*

LEADER: *But I . . .*

NP PUPPET: *When someone yells at me like you just did, there's only one thing I can do.* (Sweetly.) *I forgive you.*

(Leader holds his head in his hands and exits, followed by NP Puppet.)

GP9: How Do We Treat Them?

Cast: Ponder, Noah's Park Puppet 2

Props: Piece of candy, piece of bubblegum

PUPPET 2: *(Holds piece of candy and waves it at the kids.)* **Hey,** *(Name of a child.)* **! You look like you could use a piece of candy. Hope you find someone to give you one because you can't have mine!** *(Laughs. Puts down candy and picks up bubblegum.)* **Hey,** *(Name of another child.)* **! You look like you could use a piece of bubblegum. Hope you find someone to give you one because you can't have mine!** *(Laughs.)*

PONDER: *(Enters.)* *(Name of puppet.)* **! Stop that. You're being mean to the kids.**

PUPPET 2: **That wasn't me. It was someone else.** *(Tries to hide the bubblegum.)*

PONDER: **Now you're lying to me.**

PUPPET 2: **Aw. I was just teasing. We were having some fun.**

PONDER: *(Name of puppet.)*, **I'm surprised at you. Is that how God wants you to treat others?**

PUPPET 2: **Don't know. Didn't ask.**

PONDER: **Do you really not care?**

PUPPET 2: *(Looks repentant.)* **Well, when I think about it, I guess I DO really care.**

PONDER: **When Jesus was on earth, He treated others well because God wants us to treat each other kindly.**

PUPPET 2: **Oh. Do you mean that if I want to be like Jesus, I can't do any more mean tricks?**

PONDER: **That's right.**

PUPPET 2: **Do you mean that to be like Jesus, I should treat others the way I want to be treated?**

PONDER: **Exactly.**

PUPPET 2: **No more blowing bubbles at the pastor during church?**

PONDER: **None.**

PUPPET 2: **No more plastic chocolates for my Sunday school teacher?**

PONDER: **Definitely no more plastic chocolate candies.**

PUPPET 2: **Then I'd better get home before Mom finds the fake spider in her closet. Bye, Ponder.** *(Exit.)*

GP10: Amazing Light

Cast: Ponder, Noah's Park Puppet 2

Props: Screwdriver

Puppet 2 holds a screwdriver. Ponder enters.

PUPPET 2: *Ponder, can you help me with something?*

PONDER: *Sure.*

PUPPET 2: *When I tell you, would you turn the lights off and on?*

PONDER: *Sure.*

PUPPET 2: *Okay, turn them off.* (Lights go off.)

PONDER: *How's that?*

PUPPET 2: *Great. Now turn them on.* (Lights go on.)

PONDER: *There you go.*

PUPPET 2: *Perfect. Now turn them off.* (Lights go off.) *Super. Turn them back on.* (Lights go on.) *Now off.* (Lights go off.) *Now on.* (Lights go on.)

PONDER: *What are you fixing?*

PUPPET 2: *Nothing. Now off.* (Lights go off.) *Now on.* (Lights go on.)

PONDER: *You're not fixing anything?*

PUPPET 2: *Nope.*

PONDER: *Then why am I doing this?*

PUPPET 2: *To help me understand something. When God said, "Let there be light." It's like He said, "Okay, turn them on"—like I just did. And when God said that, the lights turned on. Isn't that cool?* (Turns to kids.) *Do you kids want to try it?* (Waits for a response.) *Say, "Off."* (Pauses to let kids say, "off." Lights go off.) *Say, "On."* (Pauses for kids. Lights go on.) *Say, "Off."* (Lights go off.) *Say, "On."* (Lights go on.) *Isn't that great how God made our world? He just said it, and it happened.*

PONDER: *But kids, I have to caution you. Don't flip the light switch on and off at home unless your Mom or Dad gives you permission.*

PUPPET 2: *What Ponder's saying is that God made day and night, but don't you try it at home!*

(Exit.)

GP11: Creation Rap

Cast: Ponder, Noah's Park Puppet 2

Props: Puppet-size sunglasses for Puppet 2

PONDER: *Why are you wearing sunglasses?*

PUPPET 2: *I'm cool.*

PONDER: *Having sunglasses on when you're inside of a building is cool?*

PUPPET 2: *It is when you're about to do a rap about how God made the world.*

PONDER: *I've got to see this.* (Stands to the side but nothing happens.) *Are you going to start rapping?*

PUPPET 2: *As soon as someone makes rap noises for me.* (Ponder begins to make rap noises. Puppet 2 begins saying the following in a rap style.) *God made water, to drink, to swim in, to bathe in, to make into mud pies, to spray at your friends, to make into water balloons and throw at your friends when they don't know you're doing it.*

PONDER: (Stops making rap noises.)(Name of puppet.)*!*

PUPPET 2: *Okay, start again.* (Ponder starts rap noises again. Puppet 2 begins speaking in rap rhythm again.) *God made air so we can breathe, walk through it, rap in it, carry sound waves, blow up balloons,* blow bubbles, carry the sound of a honking horn when you get in your parent's car when they don't know . . .

PONDER: *(Stops again.) (Name of puppet.)***!**

PUPPET 2: **Sorry. Let's go again.** *(Both begin again.)* **God made land, the sand, my man, to walk on, make mud pies, build sand castles, throw rocks down the slide.**

PONDER: *(Stops again.) (Name of puppet.)***!**

PUPPET 2: *(Keeps going without Ponder.)* **God made the sky . . .**

PONDER: **How many verses do you have?**

PUPPET 2: **Only 6,000 so far.**

PONDER: **6,000!**

PUPPET 2: **God made so much that I've just got to rap about it. Don't worry, this rap song should only take two months to sing.**

PONDER: **Oh, no.** *(Leaves.)*

PUPPET 2: *(Follows Ponder off the stage.)* **God made the sky . . .**

GP12: Changing Seasons

Cast: Ponder, Noah's Park Puppet 2

PUPPET 2: *I'm a "fall" kind of person.*

PONDER: *A what?*

PUPPET 2: *You know. A person who likes fall—
the season of the year.*

PONDER: *Oh, and you like fall the best?*

PUPPET 2: *Yes, I like autumn because leaves
change colors and the air is cool and
we roast marshmallows over bonfires . . .*

PONDER: *And school starts and you have to
wear shoes and long pants instead of
shorts . . .*

PUPPET 2: *Oh, I was wrong. What I meant to say
was that I like winter.*

PONDER: *You do?*

PUPPET 2: *Yeah, you can have snowball fights
and Christmas vacation and . . .*

PONDER: *And catch colds and wear extra
sweaters and have to dig out cars
stuck in the snow . . .*

PUPPET 2: *Oh, I was wrong. I like spring best
because new plants bud and school
break begins and you don't have to
wear a coat everywhere . . .*

PONDER: *And you have final tests at school and you go to the dentist after eating all of your Easter sweets and . . .*

PUPPET 2: *Oh, I was wrong. I like summer because I don't need shoes and I get more time off of school . . .*

PONDER: *And you can weed the garden and it gets so hot that you sweat and your ice cream melts and . . .*

PUPPET 2: *God made so many seasons.*

PONDER: *He made four seasons.*

PUPPET 2: *There has to be one that's perfect.*

PONDER: *(Laughs.)* **Only God is perfect. But He did make something GREAT in every season.**

(Exit.)

GP13: A Rhyming Creation

Cast: Ponder, Noah's Park Puppet 2

Props: Paper, pencil

Puppet 2 is onstage alone, holding a pencil and pretending to write on the paper.

PUPPET 2: *(Thinking and writing.)*

God made the trees,

God made the bees,

God made . . . keys, deaz, heez, leez . . . Okay, let's try something else. *(Crosses off what he wrote.)*

God made birds,

God made . . . curds, durds, sirds . . .

(Sighs and crosses off.)

God made the fish,

God made a dish,

God made . . .

(To the kids.) **Writing a poem about every animal God created is really hard.**

PONDER: *(Enters.)* **What are you doing,** *(Name of puppet.)***?**

PUPPET 2: **I'm making a poem for my Children's Church teacher about how God made all the animals in the world.**

PONDER: *Let me hear it.*

PUPPET 2: *No.*

PONDER: *Don't be shy.*

PUPPET 2: *I'm not being shy. I can't figure out the rhyme.*

PONDER: *Well, maybe it's time . . . to mime!*

PUPPET 2: *Mime? What's mime?*

PONDER: *It means to act out the animal without saying a word. I'll say an animal and you and the kids can act it out without a single sound. Ready?* (Puppet 2 nods yes. Then Ponder asks kids.) *Ready?* (Pause for kids to nod or shout yes.) *Okay, here goes: **Deer.*** (Pause for puppet and kids to mime.) ***Penguin.*** (Pause again.) ***Hippopotamus.*** (Pause.) ***Chicken.*** (Pause.) ***Snake.*** (Pause.)

PUPPET 2: *That was fun. Maybe my teacher will let me act them out. Because even though God made everything, I can't even make up a poem about all He did. He's amazing!*

(Exit.)

GP14: Big Plans for a Special Baby

Cast: Noah's Park Puppet, Leader

Puppet hurries over to Leader, who is reading his Bible.

NP PUPPET: *(Jumping around excitedly.)* **Big news! Big news! My aunt is going to have a baby! A new baby cousin for me! Can't talk, gotta run. I have big plans for this special baby!** *(Starts to leave.)*

LEADER: **Wait a minute! What are you doing?**

NP PUPPET: **Didn't you hear me? I'm making big plans for my new baby cousin! I have to get ready!**

LEADER: **That's exciting news. But what are YOU going to do to get ready for a baby cousin?**

NP PUPPET: **Well, um . . . that's a good question. What DO I need to get ready?** *(Thinks for a moment.)* **I know. I'll buy it a bike, and we can go riding together!**

LEADER: **Whoa,** *(Name of puppet.)***! It's great you're making plans for this special baby. But I think you're getting a little ahead of things. A tiny baby can't do much in the beginning. They just eat, sleep—and sometimes give cute little smiles!**

NP PUPPET: *Really? Well, I like the smiling part, but you mean I can't play with it? I can't make big plans?*

LEADER: *(Gives puppet a pat on the back.)* **Of course, you can,** *(Name of puppet.).* **Just make plans that would help a little, bitty baby.**

NP PUPPET: *(To audience.)* **Will YOU help me with ideas? What does a newborn baby need?** *(Puppet and Leader listen and nod to all answers called out, then continue.)* **Let's see . . . blankets, a crib, clothes, diapers . . . that's a great list! And I think MY part of the plan will be to give the new baby a stuffed animal. What do you think,** *(name of leader.)?*

LEADER: **I think that's a great plan. Did you know that God had a great plan for a special baby too? He planned to send His own Son, Jesus, to earth as a baby. And when the angel told God's plan to Mary, His mother, she was so happy that she made big plans too. She even made up a song to praise God!**

NP PUPPET: **Wow! Jesus must have been a special baby! Do you think He had a stuffed animal to hug?**

LEADER: *(Laughing.)* **I don't know. But I'm sure that whatever He had was part of God's big plan.** *(Exit.)*

GP15: Obeying Joseph's Way

Cast: Ponder the Frog, Noah's Park Puppet 2

Puppet 2 is sleeping. Ponder enters from other side.

PONDER: *(Calls.)* **Hello? Helloooo,** *(Name of Puppet 2.),* **are you there?** *(Walks over and taps Puppet 2.)* *(Name of Puppet.),* **wake up! I came to visit you.**

PUPPET 2: *(Wakes up suddenly with a big snort.)* **What? Who? Oh, Ponder! It's you. I was having the most WONDERFUL dream!**

PONDER: *(Chuckles.)* **I thought so. What was it about?**

PUPPET 2: **Hmm! What WAS I dreaming about? I can't remember. It must not have been very important or I would have remembered it, right?** *(Laughs.)*

PONDER: *(Laughs with him.)* **Probably so. Say, talking about dreaming reminds me of our Bible story in Children's Church today. Do you remember what it was?**

PUPPET 2: **Um, let's see. It was about Joseph.**

PONDER: **Right! One night an angel of the Lord came to Joseph in a dream. He told Joseph that Mary's baby was from God—a very special baby. The angel told Joseph not to be afraid, but to**

go ahead and get married to Mary. The angel even told Joseph what to name the baby—Jesus.

PUPPET 2: *And doesn't Jesus' name mean something special?*

PONDER: *Yes, it does. It means Savior. This all happened, because God promised long ago that He would send a Savior to save us from our sins.*

PUPPET 2: *Wow! I wish I could have a dream like Joseph's!*

PONDER: *Yes, it was an amazing dream. And do you know what is MORE amazing?*

PUPPET 2: *What could be more amazing than an angel talking to you in your dream?*

PONDER: *The AMAZING thing is that when Joseph woke up, he DID what the angel of the Lord told him to do! Joseph obeyed God. Joseph showed you and me how to listen to God and obey Him.*

PUPPET 2: *(Yawns big and noisily.)* **Sorry, Ponder. Talking about dreams makes me sleepy. I feel a nap coming on. Say, why did you come over to see me?**

PONDER: *(Laughs and scratches his head.)* **You know, I can't remember! Well, I'll run along and let you get back to dreaming.** *(Exits. Puppet 2 lies down again.)*

GP16: Welcome the New Baby

Cast: Ponder the Frog, Noah's Park Puppet 2

Props: A small gift-wrapped box

Ponder is onstage.

PUPPET 2: *(Very excited.)* **Ponder! Ponder! Oh, there you are! I was looking everywhere for you. I've got great news!**

PONDER: **Hi,** *(Name Puppet 2.)*. **What's going on?**

PUPPET 2: **Ponder, my aunt had her tiny baby! It's a boy, and his name is Junior. Isn't that great? You've just GOT to come and see him!**

PONDER: **That IS great news! I would love to go see Junior.**

PUPPET 2: **I have a present for him, Ponder. Do you think he'll like it?** *(Picks up a small gift-wrapped box.)*

PONDER: **What is it?**

PUPPET 2: **It's a dump truck with a stack of bananas on top. I love bananas!**

PONDER: *(Chuckles.)* **Well, he may have to wait awhile before he can play with the truck. And I'm sure he's too little to eat bananas. But his Mom and Dad will enjoy eating them. Babies ARE special. Everyone wants to give them**

a gift. It's a way of welcoming them. This reminds me of the night baby Jesus was born.

PUPPET 2: Me too, Ponder. Mary and Joseph must have been SO happy! My aunt is happy too. She made a special place for Junior—not like the old stable that baby Jesus was born in. Junior has his very own little bed and a soft white pillow. Lots of the animals from Noah's Park have come to see him.

PONDER: Imagine that! The whole park welcomes a little baby! Did you know that Jesus was welcomed too?

PUPPET 2: He was?

PONDER: Not by the animals in Noah's Park. But by other animals—and people too. Shepherds and farm animals crowded into the stable to see this little one sent from heaven. The animals shared their food box so Jesus could have a bed. And they shared their hay so that He would have something soft to lie on. Whenever we thank God for Junior, we can also thank God for His Son, Jesus.

PUPPET 2: That's a great idea. Now, come on, Ponder! Let's go to WELCOME Junior!

PONDER: Okay, let me get my gift. (Both exit.)

GP17: The Announcement

Cast: Ponder the Frog, Noah's Park Puppet 2

Props: A sign that a puppet could hold, labeled: "Come See the Sweetest, Cutest Baby in the Whole Wide World!"

Puppet 2 holds the sign, showing it to the audience.

PONDER: Hi, *(Name of Puppet 2.)*. **What's this?** *(Reads the sign aloud.)* **"Come See the Sweetest, Cutest Baby in the Whole Wide World!" Wow! What a sign!**

PUPPET 2: *(Proudly.)* **Do you like it, Ponder? I made it all by myself!**

PONDER: **You're very proud of your new cousin. You remind me of when Jesus was born. God wanted everyone to know too!**

PUPPET 2: **Did God use a sign like mine?**

PONDER: *(Chuckles.)* **No,** *(Name of puppet.)*. **God's announcement was even bigger! He lit up the whole sky with light! He sent a gazillion angels to announce the birth of Jesus. They appeared to shepherds in the field with their sheep.**

PUPPET 2: **Wow! That WAS some announcement! I bet those shepherds really wanted to see baby Jesus! But how did they know where to go?**

PONDER: **Good question. The angels told them to go to Bethlehem and look for a baby**

wrapped in cloths, lying in a manger.

PUPPET 2: *Ponder, that's too hard! That would be like saying,* **"Come to** (Name of your town.) **and find the baby with blue pajamas and yellow blanket lying in a crib."** **Nobody could find that!**

PONDER: (Laughs.) **That WOULD be hard. But God chose a simple place for Jesus to be born. God made sure that people found out about His Son! And the shepherds found baby Jesus in the manger, just as the angel had said.**

PUPPET 2: **How did everyone else find out?**

PONDER: **On their way back to the fields, the shepherds told everyone they saw! And you know what else? We also can tell others about Jesus' birth. We can help spread God's good news!**

PUPPET 2: **That's like what I'm doing with my new cousin. I'm telling everyone!**

PONDER: (Laughs.) **Yes. And while you're at it, maybe you could share the good news about Jesus' birth, too.**

PUPPET 2: **That's a good idea! Hey, Ponder, do you want to help?**

PONDER: **Sure! Let's get started!**

(Exit.)

GP18: What Can I Give Him?

Cast: Ponder the Frog, Noah's Park Puppet #2

Puppet 2 is facing offstage, pretending to study a picture hanging there.

PONDER: *Hello, (Name of Puppet 2.)! What are you looking at?*

PUPPET 2: *Hi, Ponder! I'm looking at a picture of Mary, Joseph, and Jesus with some visitors. But I'm wondering who the visitors are. They look like kings.*

PONDER: *Well, they were called wise men. They were very smart, and understood many things.*

PUPPET 2: *How did they find Jesus? And why did they go see Him, anyway?*

PONDER: *God had told His people hundreds of years before that He would send His Son. These wise men looked for clues of when God's Son would be born. When they saw the special star that God put in the sky—because they were so wise—they knew it was a clue of how to find Jesus!*

PUPPET 2: *But why did they want to find Him?*

PONDER: *Because God said that His Son would be the Savior. The birth of God's Son is pretty important! These wise men traveled for thousands of miles to find Jesus.*

PUPPET 2: *Wow! And what did they do when they found Him?*

PONDER: *(Laughs.)* **Well, the wise men brought VERY expensive presents. And they knelt down before Jesus and worshiped Him.**

PUPPET 2: *What is worship, Ponder? What did they DO to worship Jesus?*

PONDER: **The wise men spent a lot of time and effort going to see Him. They brought Him gifts. They loved Him. But most importantly, they let Jesus know that they believed He was God's own Son. And we should only worship God and His Son!**

PUPPET 2: *Ponder, how can I show Jesus that I love Him? I want to worship Him too.*

PONDER: **We can all do SOMEthing,** *(Name of Puppet #2.)* **. We can learn about Him through the Bible. We can talk with Him every day. We can sing Him praises. We can give Him our hearts.**

PUPPET 2: *That's great, Ponder. I WILL give my heart to Jesus!*

PONDER: **Good choice,** *(Name of Puppet 2.)***.** *(Exit.)*

GP19: The Play-Dough Man

Cast: Ponder the Frog, Noah's Park Puppet 2

Props: Lump of play dough, a person-shaped cookie cutter

Puppet 2 hums while playing with play dough and cookie cutter.

PUPPET 2: *Oh, boy! I can hardly wait to play with my play dough. I'm going to make a gingerbread man.* (Holds up the cookie-cutter for audience to see.)

PONDER: (Enters and clears throat noisily.) *Harrumph!*

PUPPET 2: (Throws arms up and shrieks.) *Yikes! Ponder! You startled me! I didn't hear you come in.*

PONDER: *Hi,* (Name of puppet.). *Sorry I startled you. I just wanted to watch you, my friend. What are you making with your play dough?*

PUPPET 2: (Pretending to shape play dough.) *I'm making a play dough man. He will have eyes, a nose, and a big smile when I'm done. He will also have a belt and buttons down his front. What do you think?* (Stands back proudly. Ponder looks closely.)

PONDER: *That's a good start! What else do you have planned for your little man of clay?*

PUPPET 2: *I'm going to make him a wife to keep him company, and even some little children!*

PONDER: *This reminds me of when God set out to create the world and all that was in it! What a time that must have been!*

PUPPET 2: *You mean when He created the first man and woman and all the animals?*

PONDER: *Exactly. God made man and woman with a very special plan in mind—just as you are doing with your play-dough family. God knew exactly what we were going to be like even BEFORE He started making us. Imagine that!*

PUPPET 2: *Wow! We ARE pretty special, aren't we?*

PONDER: *Yes! The Bible tells us that PEOPLE are the most special part of all of God's creation.*

PUPPET 2: *Wow!* (Pauses to think.) *Do you think the PEOPLE know that?*

PONDER: *Some of them do . . . and your little play-dough family can remind the rest of them. I need to go now, but I'll check in later to see your play dough family—when it's all finished!* (Exits.)

PUPPET 2: *Bye, Ponder. I'm going to work hard while you're gone!* (Returns to her play dough. End.)

GP20: Just-Right Jobs

Cast: Ponder, Noah's Park Puppet # 2

Ponder and Noah's Park Puppet #2 sit beside each other.

PUPPET 2: *Just look at that beaver working so hard! I bet he'll have that dam finished before dark.*

PONDER: *Just look how neat his house is! He sure is a hard worker.*

PUPPET 2: *The beaver is just right for that job. I wouldn't like being wet all the time. AND I don't have teeth like the beaver's to cut down trees.*

PONDER: *My feet could never hold onto sticks like he does, either. But I wouldn't mind the water!*

PUPPET 2: *We really are pretty different, aren't we, Ponder? From the way we look, to the kinds of jobs we do.*

PONDER: *That's right,* (Name of puppet.). ***God made each of us different and gave each of us a just-right job.***

PUPPET 2: *But I don't think MY job is very exciting.*

PONDER: *Not all jobs are exciting, but ALL jobs are important. Since the beginning of time, God planned just-right jobs for all of His creatures. Ants collect food for the winter, bees collect pollen for* honey, and squirrels gather nuts and store them. For humans, it's the same.

PUPPET 2: You mean, people have just-right jobs, too?

PONDER: That's right. Some people build houses, some plant gardens, some work in factories, and some help in parks like Noah's Park. But they ALL have a special job to do in God's world.

PUPPET 2: (Nods head.) I guess you're right, Ponder. I DO have an important job, even though sometimes it doesn't feel that way.

PONDER: (Laughs.) Just remember, whatever we do, we should do it as if we were doing it for God.

PUPPET 2: That's a great idea, Ponder! It will make it a lot more fun if I remember I'm doing my job for God! See you later, Ponder. Have fun doing YOUR job for God! (Exits.)

PONDER: (Looks up.) Thank You, God, for giving each of us a just-right job to do!

(Exit.)

GP21: Specially Created

Cast: Ponder, Noah's Park Puppet #2

Props: Small mirror on a stand, small comb

PUPPET 2: *(Stands looking in mirror, holding comb.)* **There, that's just right. I look GREAT today! Wow-ee. I don't think there's a better-looking animal around!**

PONDER: *(Enters.)* **Harrumph! I hope I'm not interrupting! You look mighty fine today,** *(Name of puppet.).* **What's up?**

PUPPET 2: **Thanks, Ponder! I think so too. Now admit it, Ponder. Have you ever seen a better-looking animal than me?** *(Keeps looking in mirror.)*

PONDER: **Let me think. That's a hard question to answer. You know, I never stop being amazed at how wonderfully we ALL are made. Our Creator sure did a great job when He created ALL of us, didn't He?**

PUPPET 2: *(Looks at Ponder.)* **What do you mean?**

PONDER: **I mean God! He sure did an awesome job when He made each one of us! Don't you agree? Just think about it. Each one of us is SO different.**

PUPPET 2: **You can say that again! And SOME of us are nicer to look at than others!**

I feel sorry for some of those animals. They're not very pretty to look at. Some of them are really funny-looking!

PONDER: *You have a point there. But I don't think I'd want to trade places with anyone else. I don't mind being a frog now, but there was a time when I did.*

PUPPET 2: *YOU wanted to be somebody else once?*

PONDER: *I sure did! I was sad when I realized I was just a plain old frog. I wanted to be a bird and ride the winds above Noah's Park, or be a strong and ferocious beast and rule the jungle!*

PUPPET 2: *Wow, Ponder. I like who you are. You're so calm and wise.*

PONDER: *Let's face it, (Name of puppet.), **frogs aren't the prettiest of God's creatures. But I've learned that God cares more about how I ACT than how I LOOK!***

PUPPET 2: *(Puts down the comb and hangs his head.)* **I guess I DO think too much about what I look like.**

PONDER: *It's never too late to change. Just remember—each one of us is special because God made each animal and person just the way they are. And, in MY opinion, (Name of puppet.), **God made YOU one good-looking animal!***

(Exit, laughing.)

GP22: Let's Get Along!

Cast: Ponder the Frog, Noah's Park Puppet #2, one
helper from the Park Patrol

Park Patrol and Puppet 2 stand near each other and argue.

PUPPET 2: *I can't believe you just splashed mud on my clean fur! Now I'll have to take another bath.*

PARK PATROL: *(Laughs.) Oh, (Name of puppet.), you're always so serious! Come on, let's play and have some fun!*

PUPPET 2: *No! You are rude AND mean! I will NOT play with you. Go away! (Turns his back on Park Patrol helper.)*

PARK PATROL: *Aw, come on. You know it's not that bad. Let's go and play a trick on someone.*

PUPPET 2: *No! Go away!*

PONDER: *(Enters.) Hello, guys! (Looks back and forth between Puppet 2 and Park Patrol helper.) Oh! Did I interrupt something?*

PUPPET 2: *(With feeling.) You sure did! That kid just gave me a mud bath AND he thinks it's funny.*

PARK PATROL: *Ponder, will you tell this animal to loosen up and have some fun?*

PONDER: *I think what we need here is a*

peacemaker!

**PUPPET 2 &
PARK PATROL:** *A what?*

PONDER: *(Pronounces clearly.)* **A peacemaker. That's someone who is willing to say, "I'm sorry" and try to get along with others.**

PUPPET 2: **It's NOT going to be me, because I didn't do anything wrong.**

PARK PATROL: *(To Ponder.)* **I didn't do anything wrong, either!** *(To Puppet 2.)* **Just because YOU happened to walk by just when I was splashing mud.**

PONDER: **The Bible says it's not right to fight. You and** *(Name of puppet.)* **are friends. Wouldn't it be sad if you lost your friendship simply because one of you was too stubborn to say, "I'm sorry?"**

PARK PATROL: **I guess you're right, Ponder. It's not much fun splashing if it makes someone else mad!** *(To Puppet 2.)* **I'm sorry,** *(Name of puppet.)*. **Will you forgive me?**

PUPPET 2: **Oh, all right! I forgive you. I'm sorry for holding a grudge. Let's be friends again!**

PONDER: **I'm proud of you two! I guess I just met a pair of peacemakers!** *(Exit.)*

GP23: We Can Give Something

Cast: Ponder the Frog, Noah's Park Puppet #2

Noah's Park Puppet #2 is crying. Ponder enters.

PONDER: *(Name of Puppet 2.),* **why are you crying? I thought you'd be out helping the other animals bring things for the new Worship Hut that we're building.**

PUPPET 2: *(Sniffing.)* **Oh, Ponder. I don't have ANYTHING to bring! All the other animals have things in their homes they can give. Or they find nice things around Noah's Park to bring. I want to help, but I don't have anything to give. I don't even have money.**

PONDER: **There, there. You don't have to cry. I'm sure there's SOME way you can help. Let me think for a minute. I wonder how Noah would work out this problem. Hmm!** *(Thinking hard.)* **I know! You can PRAY for the project.**

PUPPET 2: **Ponder, I DO pray already! But I want to GIVE something or BRING something that will help build God's Worship Hut in Noah's Park.**

PONDER: **Um, you could . . . um, you could . . .** *(Pauses to think.)* **I've got it! All the other animals are getting tired out from carrying things for the Worship**

Hut. Maybe you could stay at the Worship Hut and help organize everything as it comes in. You could help put things where they go.

PUPPET 2: *How would that be giving, Ponder?*

PONDER: *You'd be giving your time and your brains and your cheerful attitude!*

PUPPET 2: *Are those important, Ponder?*

PONDER: *Yes, they are. We each have something to give. If we don't have money or THINGS to give to God, then we give Him what we have. That might be stuff we know how to do—our talents and skills—or some encouragement and a cheerful smile!*

PUPPET 2: *I think you're right, Ponder! That's what I can give. I can be a big help to the animals who are bringing gifts to the Worship Hut! I have to get over there!*

PONDER: *I'll come too. (Exit.)*

GP24: Listen and Learn

Cast: Ponder the Frog, Noah's Park Puppet #2

Props: A small Bible

Ponder sits by an open Bible and looks at it. Noah's Park Puppet #2 approaches him timidly.

PUPPET 2: *Um, hello, Ponder. May I interrupt you for a moment?*

PONDER: *(Looks up.)* **Hello,** *(Name of puppet.).* **What are you doing today? Have you been out collecting blueberries?**

PUPPET 2: *No, Ponder. I did that yesterday. Um, Ponder, I have a question I want to ask you. I'm confused about something.*

PONDER: *Go ahead and ask me,* (Name of puppet.). *What is it?*

PUPPET 2: *Well, my mom and I went to church today. Mom told me that we were going to the "worship service." But I don't remember "worshiping." The pastor read the Bible. Then he talked about the Bible story he had just read. Then everybody prayed. I was confused. What IS worship, Ponder?*

PONDER: *That's a good question. Worship can be a lot of things. Mainly, worship is when we treat God like He is GOD! Very special!*

PUPPET 2: *Oh! That makes sense.*

PONDER: *We can treat God special by gathering with other people who love Him, like at church. We can treat God special by singing songs to praise Him. We can treat God special by reading His book—the Bible—out loud for everyone to hear. When we listen to the Bible and learn about God, that's a way to worship God too.*

PUPPET 2: *Oh, I see. So my Mom and I WERE worshiping God this morning!*

PONDER: *Yes you were—especially, if you were listening to the Bible story with your whole heart. Remember Ezra in the Bible? He read God's Word to the people of Israel. Ezra knew that hearing God's Word would help the people love God more. Loving God is a way to worship Him!*

PUPPET 2: *Oh, that's good! I'm glad I listened and learned and loved God this morning! (Pauses timidly again.)* **Um, Ponder, I have one more question.**

PONDER: *Go ahead.*

PUPPET 2: *Ponder, do you think you can worship God by eating? I love to eat!*

PONDER: *(Chuckles.)* **Well,** *(Name of puppet.),* **we'll have to talk about THAT another time.** *(Exit laughing.)*

GP25: See You at the Rock

Cast: Ponder the Frog, Leader

Ponder and Leader are talking about the kids in Children's Church.

PONDER: *It seems like some of the children that attend Children's Church are upset and worrying about things.*

LEADER: *(Looking at Ponder.)* **You know, Ponder, I think you are right. Some of the children are facing some difficult situations in their lives.**

PONDER: *I wish there were something I could do to help them. What do you think I could do to help cheer them up?*

LEADER: *Well, Ponder, all of us face difficulties at different times. I see things than can cause me to worry as I go through the day. But sometimes when I worry, I forget to pray to God. When I forget to pray, God seems very far away. Then my problems seem bigger.*

PONDER: *Does that mean you should always pray—about everything?*

LEADER: *That's right, Ponder. Praying reminds us that Jesus is right there with us. I especially like to pray with a friend or at church.*

PONDER: *Oh! So you can pray when you are alone OR with other Christians!*

LEADER: *God likes it when we worship Him— and He doesn't want us to forget to worship Him together as a group. Wouldn't it be fun to do that today, Ponder?*

PONDER: *It sure would.*

LEADER: *Here's my idea. We'll have a time of prayer with all the children today in Children's Church. They will be able to take their problems and worries to Jesus.*

PONDER: *That's a great idea! I'll feel much better if I know that the children have a way to take care of their problems! See you later!*

LEADER: *Okay, Ponder! See you at our prayer time!*

GP26: Noisy Worship

Cast: Ponder the Frog, Noah's Park Puppet #2

Props: Small toy drum set, one maraca or other rhythm instrument

Noah's Park Puppet #2 bangs away on the drum.

PONDER: *(Enters holding maraca.)* **Hello,** *(Name of Puppet 2.)***! What are you doing?**

PUPPET 2: **Hi, Ponder. I'm practicing my drums for the worship service next Sunday. Are you going to come?**

PONDER: **I sure am,** *(Name of puppet.)***. I'm going to play this.** *(Holds up instrument and plays a bit)* **I can hardly wait. We are going to make BEAUTIFUL music to praise Jesus!**

PUPPET 2: **We sure are. Ivory the elephant is going to play the recorder. I sure hope she practices a lot. I don't want her music to hurt God's ears!**

PONDER: *(Laughs.)* **I'm sure Ivory is practicing,** *(Name of puppet.)***. Shadow the raccoon is going to play the triangle. I heard also that Howler the lion will play the cymbals. All the birds in Noah's Park are practicing in the choir. I heard them singing on my way here. It's going to be great! Worshiping God with music is a good way to show God**

how much we love Him.

PUPPET 2: Let's see how we sound right now, Ponder. A one, two, three! *(Both start playing as loudly as possible for about 10 seconds, then stop.)*

PONDER: Hmm, well, that's not so bad. At least, I hope God will like it!

PUPPET 2: Ponder, I think God will love to hear us—no matter what we sound like! We just have to do our best and praise Him in our hearts as we play.

PONDER: That's right, *(Name of puppet.)*. What matters most is what we're thinking in our hearts. I want to say thank you to God for being so good to me. When I'm playing my instrument, that's what I'll say to Him.

PONDER: As I play my drums, I'm going to thank God for my family. And ALL of us—as we sing and play our instruments—can tell God how much we love Him. After all, He invented music—He's the Creator of heaven and earth.

PUPPET 2: Yes! AND don't forget—He created all the beautiful nature in Noah's Park too! Say, *(Name of puppet.)*, we'd better go. The big practice starts soon.

PONDER: You're right! We'd better go! *(Exit.)*

GP27: Just Because I Can

Cast: Ponder, Noah's Park Puppet #2

Puppet 2 looks at the ground.

PONDER: *(Enters.)* **What are you doing,** *(Name of Puppet 2.)***?**

PUPPET 2: **Watching an ant.**

PONDER: **For science class?**

PUPPET 2: **No.**

PONDER: **Because it's carrying something?**

PUPPET 2: **No.**

PONDER: **Because you want to know where it's going?**

PUPPET 2: **No.**

PONDER: **I give up. Why are you watching that ant?**

PUPPET 2: **I'm watching this ant because I'm going to squash it.**

PONDER: **Why would you do that?**

PUPPET 2: **Because.**

PONDER: **Because why?**

PUPPET 2: **Just because I can.**

PONDER: **I'm glad that Jesus isn't like that! He has the power to do anything He wants.**

PUPPET 2: *Like squashing ants?*

PONDER: *Yes. Ants and anything else. But He is so great and loves us so much that He takes care of us instead. Just because you can do something doesn't mean you should do it.*

PUPPET 2: *I don't love this ant. I don't even like it. But I won't squash it.*

PONDER: (Name of Puppet 2.), *I knew you would do the right thing.*

PUPPET 2: *Yeah. Besides, I just realized it was a piece of dirt and not an ant.*

(Exit.)

GP28: Ultimate Peek-a-Boo

Cast: Ponder, Noah's Park Puppet #2

PUPPET 2: *(To kids.)* **I love playing peek-a-boo. But no one has time to play it with me right now. Kids, will you play peek-a-boo with me?** *(Waits for kids to respond. All the kids should shout, "Yes!")* **Okay, cover your eyes with your hands. Don't peek! Now keep your hands over your eyes until I say, "peek-a-boo," okay?** *(Wait for response.)* **Wait, I didn't hear you. Are you going to keep your hands over your eyes until you hear me say, "peek-a-boo"?** *(Waits for response.)* **Promise?** *(Waits for response.)* **Here comes Ponder. Keep your hands over your eyes. And don't put them down until I say, "peek-a-boo," okay?** *(Waits for response.)*

PONDER: *(Enters.)* **Hello,** *(Name of puppet.)***.** *(Ponder looks at the kids and then at Puppet 2.)* **Why do the kids have their hands over their eyes?**

PUPPET 2: **We're getting ready to play a game.**

PONDER: **Great idea! Do you know what this reminds me of?**

PUPPET 2: **No.**

PONDER: **It reminds me of how Jesus played the**

ultimate game of peek-a-boo.

PUPPET 2: *I've never read about Jesus playing that game. I think you're teasing me.*

PONDER: *Oh yes, He did. Jesus loved two blind men so much that He showed the greatness of His power by healing their eyes.*

PUPPET 2: *That's not the same game.*

PONDER: *Think about it. It was like all these kids here with hands over their eyes. Only the blind men didn't have to put their hands over their eyes to not see. Then Jesus said they could see, just like a game of peek-a-boo.*

PUPPET 2: *You mean that when I say the word, the kids will be able to see, just as the blind men did?*

PONDER: *Yes, just like the ultimate game of peek-a-boo.*

PUPPET 2: *(Turns to kids.)* **Okay, kids. Are you ready?** *(Waits for response.)* **PEEK-A-BOO! That was fun. Let's do it again! Cover your eyes again. PEEK-A-BOO! One more time. PEEK-A-BOO! That was great! You are wonderful peek-a-boo players. Thanks for playing with me.**

(Exit.)

GP29: How Much Do You Trust Me?

Cast: Ponder, Noah's Park Puppet #2

Ponder and Puppet 2 are in the middle of a discussion.

PONDER: *That sounds crazy.*

PUPPET 2: *No really. Fall back, and I'll catch you. You don't trust me very much.*

PONDER: *What's falling down have to do with trust?*

PUPPET 2: *It's a game to help build trust.*

PONDER: *Trust does need to be built, but you don't build it by falling down.*

PUPPET 2: *That's the point. You won't fall down. If you fall backward and I catch you, then the next time I tell you something, you'll be more likely to trust that what I say is true.*

PONDER: *That's a big "if."*

PUPPET 2: *Come on, Ponder. Just try it.*

PONDER: *Well, okay. (Ponder turns his back to Puppet 2 and begins to fall. Ponder stops.) You ARE going to catch me, aren't you?*

PUPPET 2: *Of course.*

PONDER: *(Turns, starts to fall, stops, turns back to Puppet 2.)* **Just making sure that you're still there.**

PUPPET 2: **I haven't moved. Trust me.**

PONDER: **How do I get myself into things like this?** *(Turns, falls, and puppet 2 catches him.)* **You caught me!**

PUPPET 2: **Yes, I did. You're heavier than I thought you would be.**

PONDER: **You caught me just as God will catch US when we ask Him. Jesus wants us to trust Him like I had to trust you.**

PUPPET 2: **That's cool. And just so you know. I trust you too.** *(Without warning, Puppet 2 falls toward Ponder but misses and lands behind the stage. Crashing noise is heard.)*

PONDER: *(Looks down at fallen puppet.)* **There's something to be said about where you put your trust. That looks like it hurts. Hmmm, I'd better help.** *(Walks down to where Puppet #2 fell.)*

GP30: Where's the Answer?

Cast: Ponder, Noah's Park Puppet #2

PUPPET 2: *How old are you, Ponder?*

PONDER: *Old enough to remember the ark.*

PUPPET 2: *You must know everything.*

PONDER: *Not everything, but I do know a lot. Or if I don't know something, often I'll know where I can find the answer.*

PUPPET 2: *Really? Okay, here's a test. Who is the tallest person in the world?*

PONDER: *I don't know, but you can find the answer in a book called* **The Guinness Book of World Records.**

PUPPET 2: *What is the weather supposed to be like today?*

PONDER: *I don't know but you can turn on the television for the news and a weather person will tell you what the weather will probably be like today.*

PUPPET 2: *How do you spell "Children's Church"?*

PONDER: *I can tell you, but you should look it up in a dictionary yourself.*

PUPPET 2: *I'll do it later. Here's hard question. How do you learn more about God?*

PONDER: *In the Bible, through prayer, and in church.*

PUPPET 2: *That's more than one answer.*

PONDER: *God is so great and loves us so much that He decided to give us many ways to learn about Him.*

PUPPET 2: *Cool. How about this question: What day did Walla Walla win their Independence and the one-eyed, green and orange frog stop singing?*

PONDER: *(Ponder looks at Puppet 2 and then at the kids and back at the Puppet 2.)* **You can only find the answer to that one in your dreams,** *(Name of puppet.)***. Only in your dreams.**

GP31: Responses

Cast: Ponder, Noah's Park Puppet #2

PUPPET 2: *Do you want to play a fun game that a friend taught me? I'll say a word and you say the first thing that comes to your mind.*

PONDER: *Okay.*

PUPPET 2: *Pink.*

PONDER: *Water.*

PUPPET 2: *What does water have to do with the color pink?*

PONDER: *I have some pink flowers in a planter at home that I have to water.*

PUPPET 2: *Oh. I guess that's okay. The next word is, "Go."*

PONDER: *Store.*

PUPPET 2: *Flies.*

PONDER: *Lunch.*

PUPPET 2: *Hear.*

PONDER: *Do.*

PUPPET 2: *This game doesn't work. These words are supposed to go TOGETHER somehow.*

PONDER: *Let's see. You said, "Go," and I said, "Store." I have to GO to the STORE* after church to buy a get-well card for a friend. Those two words go together.

PUPPET 2: Okay. But what about "flies" and "lunch"?

PONDER: I always eat flies for lunch, at least whenever I can catch them.

PUPPET 2: Yuck!

PONDER: I AM a frog, you know.

PUPPET 2: But what about "hear" and "do"?

PONDER: Oh, "hear" and "do" are easy. Jesus wants us to really HEAR what He says and then DO it.

PUPPET 2: That makes sense.

PONDER: Most things do with God.

GP32: No One Likes Me

Cast: Ponder, Noah's Park Puppet #2

Puppet 2 is onstage.

PONDER: *(Hurries in calling name of Puppet 2.)* **You're in big trouble!**

PUPPET 2: **Go ahead and yell. I deserve it. I am so sorry.** *(Sniffles, begins to cry.)*

PONDER: *(Sighs.)* **Why did you smear mud all over the hallway out there?** *(Points to hallway outside of classroom.)*

PUPPET 2: **It's okay if you're mad at me. Everyone else is. I didn't clean my room like I told my mother I would. I went to play in a mud hole instead. My mom is really mad at me.**

PONDER: **Did you tell her you were sorry?**

PUPPET 2: **Yes, and I picked up my room, but she's still upset. I should have done it when I told her I would. Then a friend came by and wanted to play with me, but there wasn't enough room in the mud hole, so I told him NO! I wanted the mud hole for myself. Now he doesn't want to be my friend anymore.**

PONDER: **That wasn't very nice of you, was it?**

PUPPET 2: No. I went to his house to say I was sorry, but he chased me down the road!

PONDER: Oh, my!

PUPPET 2: As I was running, I decided to hide from him. I ran into the church hallway and got it all messy. I was just trying to find a place to hide. (Sighs.) No one likes me right now.

PONDER: Jesus still loves you even when no one else does. He'll listen to what happened, just as I did.

PUPPET 2: Sometimes I mess up even when I don't mean to.

PONDER: Tell you what, let's get some sponges and water and go clean up the hallway.

PUPPET 2: You still like me?

PONDER: Yes, and even better, I still love you. And best of all, so does Jesus. (Both exit, arm in arm.)

GP33: The Real Kind of King

Cast: Ponder, Noah's Park Puppet #2

Props: Paper crown to fit Puppet 2

PUPPET 2: *(Wearing crown.)* **You there. Come here!**

PONDER: *(Enters.)* **Who, me?**

PUPPET 2: **Yes, come here. I have no one else to boss around right now.**

PONDER: *(Name of puppet.)*, **what are you doing?**

PUPPET 2: **I am not** *(puppet's name.)*. **I am king for the day. Now go run in a circle.**

PONDER: **Why would I want to do that?**

PUPPET 2: **Because I'm the king and you have to obey me. Jump up and down.**

PONDER: *(Name of puppet.)*, **that's not what a king does.**

PUPPET 2: **Yes, it is. Kings boss people around. Stand on your head.**

PONDER: **No, you're wrong. Jesus is our King. He shows us what a king is like. What do you think He did?**

PUPPET 2: **He could have bossed people around.**

PONDER: **Yes, He COULD have, but He DIDN'T. He served others.**

PUPPET 2: **He served others? But He is the King. He didn't have to.**

PONDER: *Exactly. He and His friends showed His love by helping others.*

PUPPET 2: *So, to be a good king, I should show love to others and serve them?*

PONDER: *Exactly.*

PUPPET 2: *(Sighs.)* **Okay.** *(Turns to leave.)*

PONDER: *Where are you going?*

PUPPET 2: *I commanded Howler to clean my room and do my chores. I'd better go help him.*

PONDER: *Good idea.*

(Exit.)

GP34: Not Giving Up

Cast: Ponder, Noah's Park Puppet #2

PONDER: *(Looks off to the side and shouts.)* **Go, team, go! You can win this soccer game!**

PUPPET 2: *(Runs onstage to Ponder, crying and holding arm.)* **I hurt my arm. Now I can't run.**

PONDER: **You can't run because you hurt your arm?**

PUPPET 2: *(Crying.)* **Yes.**

PONDER: **But the whole soccer team is counting on you. Are you sure that you're not just sad because we're losing the game?**

PUPPET 2: **I'm sure.** *(Puppet switches arms.)* **My arm hurts, and now I can't run.**

PONDER: **Wasn't it your other arm that was hurting?**

PUPPET 2: *(Puppet switches back.)* **Yes. Now they both hurt.**

PONDER: **Hmmm, do you remember the story about how Jesus died on the cross?**

PUPPET 2: **Yes.**

PONDER: **What do you think would have happened if Jesus had died and then just said, "I'm too tired. I'm going to stay right here in this tomb. Those people out there were all mean to me when**

I was on the cross. I'm not going back out there ever again."

PUPPET 2: *Nothing.*

PONDER: *That's right. Nothing would have happened. He would have stayed dead, and we would not be able to go to heaven. Jesus didn't remain dead, though. He rose from the dead.*

PUPPET 2: *I don't understand.*

PONDER: *It's a little like what you're doing right now. You're giving up because things look bad. And if you do, we'll lose this soccer game for sure.*

PUPPET 2: *And if I go back into the game? Will we win?*

PONDER: *I don't know. In three days, Jesus showed His love by rising from the dead. If He could do that, maybe you could show your friends how much you love them by going back into the game.*

PUPPET 2: *(Nods.)* *You're right. I'd be letting the team down. After all, I don't have to rise from the dead. I just have to play soccer. (Runs offstage.)* *Hey, team! Wait for me!*

GP35: Da Best

Cast: Ponder, Puppet 2

Note: Where indicated, fill in the name of the animal that Noah's Park Puppet #2 is, such as "camel" or "rhino."

Puppet 2 is center stage. Ponder is at the side, listening.

PUPPET 2: *I am da (Name of animal puppet.)! I am da best (Name of animal.) in the world!*

PONDER: *(Comes over to Puppet #2.) You're joking, (Puppet 2's name.), aren't you? (Puppet 2 shakes its head no.) You think you're the best of all the (Name of animal.), all by yourself?*

PUPPET 2: *Yeah. I am a loner. I am da loner (Name of animal.). I am da best loner (Name of animal.) in the world!*

PONDER: *And no one helped you to get where you are today?*

PUPPET 2: *What do you mean?*

PONDER: *If you're the best, you probably have great parents.*

PUPPET 2: *I do. Mine are the very best.*

PONDER: *And good teachers.*

PUPPET 2: *Of course.*

PONDER: *And really nice friends, and a wonderful Children's Church teacher and neighbors.*

PUPPET 2: *Without a doubt.*

PONDER: *In other words, if you are the best (Name of animal.) in the world, it's only because others have taught you how to be the best.*

PUPPET 2: *Ponder, you are so smart. How did you know all of this?*

PONDER: *I know that God gives us people to teach us His ways. And I know that Jesus wants us to learn from wise people. When it comes to being the very best, Jesus is definitely "da best!" (Puppet 2 nods.) Now, (Name of Puppet 2.), I think it's time you were taught a lesson . . .*

PUPPET 2: *Not a lecture! What if I say, "Jesus is da best," and not, "I am da best"? Will that stop the lecture?*

PONDER: *It will.*

PUPPET 2: *Okay. Jesus is da best! He is da best in the whole world! (Marches offstage repeating it, followed by Ponder.)*

GP36: Helpfully Clean

Cast: Ponder, Puppet 2, Leader

Props: Small leaves *(loosely attached to Puppet 2)*, comb, washcloth

Leader and Ponder enter from opposite sides, looking all around.

LEADER: *(Calls.) (Name of Puppet 2.)***! Where are you?**

PONDER: *(Calls.) (Name of Puppet 2.)***! Where are you?**

PUPPET 2:   *(Enters, covered with leaves.)* **Here I am.**

LEADER: **What happened to you?**

PUPPET 2:   **I've been playing in the dirt and leaves. I made a really cool fort.**

PONDER: **Your grandmother's here. You have to go home right now.**

PUPPET 2:   **Oh no! I forgot. Mom told me not to play rough because Grandma was coming. What am I going to do?**

LEADER: **Come here. We'll help brush you off.** *(Leader and Ponder use their hands to brush the leaves off Puppet 2.)*

PUPPET 2:   **Ow! Ow! That hurts.**

PONDER: **I'll comb your fur.** *(Ponder picks up comb and combs Puppet #2.)*

PUPPET 2: *Ooch! Ouch! You're getting too many tangles.*

LEADER: *Let's get this smudge off of your face.* (Leader picks up washcloth, pretends to spit on it to moisten it, and rubs face of Puppet #2.)

PUPPET 2: *Oooo, yuck! You spit.*

(Leader and Ponder stand back and look at Puppet 2.)

PONDER: *You look great.*

PUPPET 2: *I do? You're great friends. I wish I could pay you back.*

LEADER: *Don't even think about paying us back. Friends help each other.*

PONDER: *Just as Jesus' friends helped others, we like helping you. Now get going. Your grandmother is waiting.*

PUPPET 2: *Thanks, guys!* (Runs off.) *Grandma! Grandma! Your favorite grandchild is here! And I'm all clean!* (End.)

GP37: Great Family Teachers

Cast: Ponder, NP Puppet #2, Leader

Leader teaches as Ponder and Puppet 2 listen onstage.

LEADER: *(To the kids.)* **In the beginning, God created the heavens and the earth.**

PUPPET 2: I know that!

PONDER: Shh!

PUPPET 2: But I know that. My grandma told me how God made the world.

LEADER: God did create a world for us. As a matter of fact, after God made an unbelievable world for us, only then did He create human beings.

PUPPET 2: I know that!

PONDER: Shhhhh, *(Name of Puppet 2.)***!**

PUPPET 2: But I know that already. My dad told me how God created human beings.

LEADER: And Adam and Eve were the very first people.

PUPPET 2: I know that!

PONDER: Shh, shh, shh, *(Name of Puppet 2.)***! Be quiet!**

PUPPET 2: But I know that already too. My mom told me.

PONDER: *(Name of Puppet 2.),* **be quiet. It's not polite to call out when the teacher's teaching.**

LEADER: **That's okay, Ponder. I'm glad to hear what** *(Name of Puppet #2.)* **is saying. Families do help us know about Jesus. It sounds like** *(Name of Puppet #2.)***'s family is doing a great job.**

PONDER: **You're right.**

LEADER: **After all, Jesus' friends help one another and that includes families.**

PUPPET 2: **Does that mean I can talk whenever I want now?**

**PONDER &
LEADER:** **Definitely not!** *(End.)*

GP38: Working Together

Cast: Ponder, Puppet 2, Leader

Ponder and Puppet 2 are onstage.

PUPPET 2: ***Let's work on a routine that*** *(Name of Leader.)* ***will like. He looks like he could use a smile.***

PONDER: ***You're right. Okay. Let's try this:***

High five! *(Puppets high-five each other.)*

High five! *(Puppets high-five each other with other hand.)*

Low five! *(Both puppets lean down and give a low high-five with both hands.)*

Back five! *(Both puppets turn around and hit their backs together.)*

Bow! *(Both puppets face each other again, bow, and hit their heads.)*

PUPPET 2: ***That's a great routine. Let's practice it again, but faster. Ready?*** *(Both puppets do the whole routine again but faster.)* ***One more time—and faster!*** *(Both puppets do the whole routine again really fast.)*

PONDER: *(Gasps and staggers.)* ***That's enough. I can't do another slap. I'm completely worn out.***

LEADER: *(Enters.)* **Hello, Ponder and** *(Name of Puppet 2.).* **What's going on?**

PUPPET 2: *(To Ponder.)* **Are you ready? Let's do it.**

PONDER: *(Still gasping.)* **I can't. I've got to catch my breath.**

PUPPET 2: **But that will spoil everything!**

LEADER: **What's the matter,** *(Name of Puppet #2.)***?**

PUPPET 2: **We wanted to help make you happy. We came up with a routine to make you smile.**

PONDER: **But we overdid it on the practice.**

LEADER: **I'm touched. That was so nice of you. Just knowing that you cared enough about me to try and do something nice makes me feel good. Do you know that Jesus' friends worked together, just like you two? By working together, they were able to help one another.**

PUPPET 2: **Really?**

LEADER: **Really.**

PUPPET 2: **I had no idea that Jesus' friends even knew how to do high-five routines.**

PONDER: *(Groans.) (End.)*

GP39: New Friends

Cast: Ponder, Puppet 2

Note: Only call on children who are comfortable being in front of the group.

Ponder stands in center stage; Puppet 2 sits on the side of the stage.

PONDER: *Hello, (Name of a child.). My name is Ponder. Come here and shake my hand. (Wait for child to come up and shake Ponder's hand.) It's nice to meet you. Did you know that Jesus is my friend? I know He loves me a lot. Did you know He loves you, too? (Wait for child to answer.) Thanks for telling me. You can sit down now. I sure enjoyed meeting you.*

PONDER: *Hello, (Name of a child.). My name is Ponder. Come here and shake my hand. (Wait for child to come up and shake Ponder's hand.) It's nice to meet you. Did you know that Jesus is my friend? I know He loves me a lot. Did you know He loves you, too? (Wait for child to answer.) Thanks for telling me. You can sit down now. I sure enjoyed meeting you.*

PUPPET 2: *(Jumps up and down, waving arms.) Ponder! Ponder! Call me next. Me! Me! Call me! Over here, Ponder!*

PONDER: *(Laughs.)* **But** *(Name of Puppet #2.),* **you already know who Jesus is.**

PUPPET 2: **But I want to TELL everyone that I do. I want everyone to know that Jesus is my friend.**

PONDER: **That's a good thing,** *(Name of Puppet #2.).* **Right now, though, I was meeting new friends. Sometimes it's good to tell new friends about Jesus.**

PUPPET 2: **Oh. Well, if you won't call on me, maybe you'd let me be the one to call on the kids?**

PONDER: **Okay,** *(Name of Puppet #2.).*

PUPPET 2: *(To center stage.)* **Hello,** *(Name of a child.).* **My name is** *(Name of Puppet #2.).* **Come here and shake my hand.** *(Wait for child to come up and shake Puppet's hand.)* **It's nice to meet you. Jesus is my friend. I know He loves me a lot. Did you know He loves you, too?** *(Wait for child to answer.)* **Thanks for telling me. You can sit down now. I enjoyed meeting you.** *(Pauses to look at Ponder, then looks at the kids.)* **Now I'm going to tell everyone about how much Jesus means to me. When I was born . . .**

PONDER: *(Warning.)* **Now, now,** *(Name of Puppet #2.)!*

PUPPET 2: **Just kidding.** *(Exits laughing.)*

GP40: Lots of Care

Cast: Ponder the Frog and Noah's Park Puppet #2

Ponder pretends to bask in the sun.

PUPPET 2: *(Enters.)* **Good morning, Ponder! Have I got good news for you!**

PONDER: **Good morning to you,** *(Name of puppet.)*. **What could be better than basking in the sun on my favorite lily pad?**

PUPPET 2: **Well, now. Mrs. Fox just gave birth to six healthy kits. AND they all look like their daddy. Mrs. Skunk has a new set of twins! The lions in Cozy Cave have two new cubs also. The whole jungle is full of new life!**

PONDER: **Well, that IS good news. Have you seen Mr. and Mrs. Monkey? How are they doing with their little brood of baby monkeys?**

PUPPET 2: **They're very busy! Yesterday I saw Mr. Monkey jumping from tree to tree, gathering food to feed his big family. But he was happy to have food to gather!**

PONDER: *(Laughs.) (Name of puppet.)*, **you are the best news carrier I know. It's great that you're friends with everyone. You can learn first-hand how all of God's**

creatures are doing!

PUPPET 2: Thanks, Ponder. I love seeing how God takes care of each family. It's amazing to see how He gives food and water for each one.

PONDER: Yes, and He also gives a good place for each family to build a nest or den. And He keeps us safe from harm so our little ones can grow up strong. God really does take good care of us.

PUPPET 2: That's for sure. Hey, I just got an idea! Let's go over to Mrs. Fox's den and offer to play with her little ones while she looks for food. That would be a great help to her—and WE can have fun playing with those cute little kits.

PONDER: Good idea! Let's go! (Exit.)

GP41: Wonderful Water

Cast: Ponder the Frog, Noah's Park Puppet #2, a Leader

Props: A small paper fan attached to a hand of each puppet OR an oscillating fan on a stand blowing cool air on the puppets

The puppets are standing in front of the fan to cool off.

PUPPET 2: *I can't believe we haven't had rain in nearly a month!*

PONDER: *Yes! It's been very hot. The pond is nearly dried up.*

PUPPET 2: *I haven't been able to take a bath in a week—my fur is loosing its shine. And I haven't had a drink for a whole day!*

PONDER: *We'll just have to be careful not to waste water. Look! Here comes* (Name of Leader.). *Maybe she will know what we should do.* (Turns toward Leader.) *Hello,* (Name of Leader.).

LEADER: (Enters.) *Hello, Ponder. Hello,* (Name of Puppet #2.). *Boy, what a nice fan. It really helps to cool off!*

PUPPET 2: *It IS nice to cool off when it's s-s-so hot and d-d-dry!* (Suddenly starts to cry.) *What will we do if our pond dries up? It hasn't rained in so long! Look, it's all muddy and not good for drinking. What will we drink? We might die!*

LEADER: (Puts arm around Puppet #2.) *Now, now,*

(Name of puppet.), **don't cry. Remember, God has promised to take care of us.**

PUPPET 2: **Do you think God will give us enough water for a nice long bath?**

LEADER: **I'm not sure about the bath, but I know God can provide water to drink. Remember the Bible story about the Israelites? They wandered in the hot, dry desert, but couldn't find any water.**

PONDER: **I remember that story. They started complaining to Moses, didn't they?**

LEADER: **Yes, but Moses prayed to God. God gave them water out of a rock! God cares for us too. Maybe God will send some rain for us.**

PUPPET 2: **I'm sorry, I was complaining just like the people of Israel.**

PONDER: **Me, too. I doubted God's care for us.** (A sound of thunder is heard offstage.) **Hey! What's that?**

PUPPET 2: **I think it was thunder! Maybe we'll have a rainstorm! God is taking care of us!**

LEADER: **I think you're right.** (Looks at children.) **Boys and girls, let's pray right now and thank God for taking care of us.**

PONDER: **Let's go down by the pond so we can watch it fill with rain!** (All exit.)

GP42: God's Good Care

Cast: Ponder the Frog, Noah's Park Puppet #2

Puppet 2 sits, looking sad.

PONDER: *Hello, (Name of puppet.). Say! What's wrong? You look sad.*

PUPPET 2: *Hi, Ponder. I am sad. My favorite aunt is moving. She got a new job.*

PONDER: *Oh! I'm sorry to hear that. Where is she moving to?*

PUPPET 2: *It's a long way from here! I don't want her to move. I like the way she helps me learn Bible stories.*

PONDER: *I'm sure you'll miss her. I know you feel sad right now—but remember Abraham! He learned that God is with us wherever we go! He'll be with your aunt.*

PUPPET 2: *I forgot about Abraham. God asked him to move too, didn't He?*

PONDER: *Yes! And Abraham obeyed God. God loved Abraham and had a good plan for him. God took good care of Abraham and his whole family.*

PUPPET 2: *Do you think God will take care of my aunt, too?*

PONDER: *I KNOW God will take care of your aunt. Trust in God,* (Name of puppet.), *and you'll feel better. Just think, when you visit your aunt, you might make new friends! Or she might find some fun, new foods for you to try!*

PUPPET 2: (Laughs.) *Thanks, Ponder. I'm feeling better already. You know, I think my aunt might like it if I tell her a Bible story—the one about Abraham.*

PONDER: *I think she might like that too.*

PUPPET 2: *See you later, Ponder!* (Exits.)

PONDER: (To children.) *And remember, God is always with YOU, too!* (Exits.)

GP43: God's Promises

Cast: Ponder the Frog, Noah's Park Puppet #2

Props: A few small branches and crumpled paper to simulate the mess after a storm

PUPPET 2: *(Looks around.)* **What a mess! That storm tore branches right off the trees. I don't think Noah's Park will EVER look the same again!**

PONDER: *(Enters.)* **Oh, there you are,** *(Name of Puppet #2.).* **I've been looking for you. I'm glad to see that you made it through the storm all right.**

PUPPET 2: **Yes, I'm okay! How about you, Ponder? I thought the wind might have blown you away!**

PONDER: *(Chuckles.)* **No, the wind didn't blow me away. But my favorite lily pad got blown right out of the pond. Have you seen it?**

PUPPET 2: **No. Just look at this mess, Ponder! Will Noah's Park ever look beautiful again? Do you think God will destroy the earth again as He did in the days when Noah was alive?**

PONDER: **Do you remember all the stories I've told you about how God used an ark to save Noah and the animals from the big flood? Do you especially**

remember the part about the rainbow?

PUPPET 2: *(Excitedly, then confused.)* **Yeah! I do! I remember! Um, I remember there was a rainbow after the flood, but I don't remember how it got there or why.**

PONDER: **God put that first rainbow in the sky. He put it there for a special reason.**

PUPPET 2: *(Excitedly, then confused.)* **Oh! I remember now! God gave a promise with the rainbow! It was . . . Uh, . . .**

PONDER: *(Chuckles.)* **God's promise was that He would never destroy the earth again with a flood. And the best part is that God ALWAYS keeps His promises.**

PUPPET 2: **But, Ponder, what about all this mess and the terrible storm?**

PONDER: **God kept His promise. Noah's Park didn't flood. And God took care of us during the storm. The Bible is full of God's promises. And He's kept each of them. So you don't have to be afraid!**

PUPPET 2: **I feel a lot better.** *(Looks around again.)*

PONDER: **And don't worry about Noah's Park. Together, we can clean it up. And God will make everything grow again!**

PUPPET 2: **You're right, Ponder. Let's get to work. I can't wait to see Noah's Park bloom again!** *(They exit with a branch.)*

GP44: The Sharing Surprise

Cast: Ponder the Frog, Noah's Park Puppet #2, a Leader

Props: One bunch of bananas, a cluster of grapes, "puppet-size" pillow or chair

PUPPET 2: *(Leaning back on pillow or chair.)* **Oh! What am I going to do? I'm getting hungry, and with my sprained ankle, how can I look for fruit to eat? I can't stand or walk! I might starve to death!** *(Starts to cry.)*

LEADER: *(Enters with bunch of bananas.)* **Hello, (Name of puppet.). Hey, have you been crying? Cheer up! Look what I brought you. I heard the news that you hurt your ankle and can't walk.**

PUPPET 2: *(Sniffling.)* **Yes! And how am I going to get my food?** *(Suddenly stops and points to the bananas.)* **What's that?**

LEADER: **These are for you! Bananas!**

(Before she can respond, Ponder enters carrying grapes.)

PONDER: **Hello, little friend! Look what I brought you! How do you feel today? Does your ankle hurt very much?**

PUPPET 2: **Oh, Ponder! I feel just awful. What is that you brought me?**

PONDER: **Some grapes to cheer you up. I hope my visit will make you feel better, too.**

PUPPET 2: *Thanks, Ponder. (Name of Leader.) brought me some bananas. Yummy! I was just getting hungry. I was thinking about how I was going to get my food. Thank you both so much!*

LEADER: *Oh, that's okay. Can you play yet?*

PUPPET 2: *No! I can't walk for a while. The doctor told me to keep my foot up and rest it. Why did you guys share your bananas and grapes with me? That was a nice thing to do.*

PONDER: *Well, God wants us to share what we have with others.*

LEADER: *I know you love bananas. So I wanted to share some with you. It was fun thinking about surprising you with them. Did it cheer you up to see us today?*

PUPPET 2: *It sure did! I love surprises.*

PONDER: *God is pleased when we share with others. I'm glad we could share with you today. Come on! Lets play "Go Fish!" We can cheer (Name of puppet.) up some more while we play. (End.)*

GP45: Let's Get Along

Cast: Ponder the Frog, a Park Patrol Helper

Ponder and Park Patrol Helper enter from opposite sides.

PONDER: *Hi, (Name of Park Patrol.)! How's it going? Do you like being in the Park Patrol?*

PK PATROL: *Hi, Ponder. Yeah, I do . . . MOST of the time. But this week things aren't going so well. I have a BIG problem.*

PONDER: *That's too bad. Tell me your problem, and maybe together we can figure out what to do.*

PK PATROL: *Okay, Ponder. I really like some of the jobs I get to do in the Park Patrol. But there are two other kids who want the same jobs. So they're always doing them before I can get to them—even when it's not their turn. It's not fair!*

PONDER: *Yes, I can see that this is a problem. Getting along with others is not always easy. Sometimes it's harder to get along with the kids that we see all the time. We have to ask God for help with getting along.*

PK PATROL: *I need God to help me, for sure! I was getting ready to yell at these kid and call them names a little* *while ago. What do YOU think I should do, Ponder?*

PONDER: *Well, God knows that fighting doesn't solve our problems. It only makes them worse! God wants us to care for others by getting along with them—even kids we sometimes don't like. So, I think you should pray first.*

PK PATROL: *Do you think God will help? Do you think He cares? Do you think He'll get rid of those kids I don't like?*

PONDER: *(Laughs.)* **Well,** *(Name of Park Patrol.),* **I** *don't think God's going to "get rid" of anybody! But God does promise to help us know what is right to do. He can help you learn patience so you don't fight with the other Park Patrols. God also gives us grown-ups to help us with our problems. AND, yes, I do know that God cares very much about you and your problems— any problem you have.*

PK PATROL: *That makes me feel better. I think I WILL talk it over with God. Maybe every day! Maybe I CAN learn to get along with the other Park Patrol kids.*

PONDER: **Good choice,** *(Name of Park Patrol Helper.).* **I know it will make a difference.** *(Exit.)*

GP46: Forgiving Others Can Be Hard

Cast: Ponder the Frog, Noah's Park Puppet #2

NP Puppet #2 is talking with Ponder.

PUPPET 2: *I can't believe they were so mean, Ponder! Just look at me! I have bruises! Screech and Shadow were tossing coconuts, and they threw some at me on purpose!*

PONDER: *Well, I can see you sure got bruised. This looks like another one of Shadow's bright ideas! Sometimes his habit of playing tricks on people gets a little out of hand. So, they were throwing coconuts, were they?*

PUPPET 2: *Yes. AND I got dirt in my eye—and it really hurts! Now I'm dirty AND hurt AND mad. I'm never going to play with those two again! Never!*

PONDER: *Now calm down. Screech and Shadow DID do something wrong. I'm very disappointed in them. Sometimes our friends do disappoint us. This reminds me a little of Joseph in the Bible. His brothers were pretty mean to him, too. Do you remember what happened to him?*

PUPPET 2: *Of course, I do. They sold Joseph as a slave to work hard in a country far away from his family. What a terrible thing they did!*

PONDER: *Yes, they did a very wrong thing. But the part we need to remember is that God made something good come from it. Joseph took his hurts to God in prayer. He forgave his brothers.*

PUPPET 2: *Ponder, how COULD Joseph forgive his brothers? They were so mean to him.*

PONDER: *It wasn't easy for him, I'm sure! But Joseph loved God and wanted to please Him. God helped Joseph to forgive his brothers. God can help YOU forgive Screech and Shadow.*

PUPPET 2: *Ponder . . . I really don't FEEL like forgiving Screech and Shadow. But I DO want to obey God. I love Him, and I know He has forgiven me for what I'VE done wrong. So I'll forgive my friends when they aren't very nice to me—even Screech and Shadow.*

PONDER: *That's good thinking,* (Name of puppet.). *God will help you, and you'll see that this is the best thing to do.*

PUPPET 2: *Hey! I think I hear Screech and Shadow coming this way. I'll talk to them now. I want to do this right!* (Voices heard offstage. Puppets exit.)

GP47: Looking for Kindness

Cast: Ponder the Frog, Noah's Park Puppet #2

NP Puppet #2 sits and pretends to watch animal friends walk past. She shakes her head no after each one passes. Ponder enters.

PUPPET 2: *I wonder where they could be!*

PONDER: *Hello, (Name of puppet.). What are you looking for?*

PUPPET 2: *Hi, Ponder! I'm looking for someone to be kind to! I can't find anybody though. Look, there's Ivory. Hi, Ivory! (Both wave.) She must be having trouble finding blueberries—they're her favorite.*

PONDER: *Why are you looking for someone to be kind to?*

PUPPET 2: *I learned at church about King David and Mah-flib-o-Oh! You know, the boy who couldn't walk well because he hurt his legs and his grandfather had been the old king and he was an enemy of David's and . . .*

PONDER: *(Chuckling.) Yes, (Name of puppet.). I know who you mean. King David was looking for someone to be kind to, and he found Meph-ibo-sheth [muh-fib-o-sheth]. Look, there's Mrs. Monkey with her baby monkeys.*

(*Waves.*) **I bet she'd like some help with those busy kids!**

PUPPET 2: **Yeah, but back to my problem. Because of that story about David and Mah-fibby-ah-what's-his-name, now I'M looking for someone to be kind to, too.** (*Calling and waving.*) **Hi, Howler! Looks like he needs some help getting knots out of his mane.**

PONDER: **Let's think about the meaning of the story. It means that God wants you to show kindness to EVERYone—not looking all day for just one person.**

PUPPET 2: **You mean, the people I could be kind to could be right here in front of me?**

PONDER: **That's right.** (*Waves.*) **Hi, Shadow!** (*To Puppet 2.*) **Shadow sure looks lonely.**

PUPPET 2: **Hey! I got it! I've got an idea! I can be kind to Shadow by keeping him company. Maybe Shadow and I can be kind TOGETHER by helping Mrs. Monkey with her kids! And we can be kind to Howler by helping him comb his tangled mane! And I can be kind to Ivory by sharing some of my blueberries with her!**

PONDER: **I think you "got it." You've got a great idea on how to be kind.**

PUPPET 2: (*Calling.*) **Shadow! Hey, Shadow, wait up!** (*Exits.*)

GP48: A Good Chance to Help

Cast: Ponder the Frog, Noah's Park Puppet #2, a Leader

Props: One birdhouse, two "puppet-size" paintbrushes

Ponder and Puppet 2 are holding the paintbrushes and taking turns "painting" the birdhouse.

PUPPET 2: *Painting is fun! I'm glad we decided to help Flutter paint her birdhouse.*

PONDER: *Me, too! Painting IS fun! I'm glad we could help Flutter today.*

(Leader enters.)

LEADER: *Hello, everyone! You two are sure working hard. It looks like Flutter will have a brand-new house soon. She'll be so happy.*

PUPPET 2: *We wanted Flutter to know that we care about her. Painting a house by yourself is a big job!*

PONDER: *That's right, (Name of Leader.). Flutter is so busy flying messages for Noah's Park that she doesn't have much time to paint! Since she helps us with our messages, we decided to help her with her house!*

LEADER: *That's a special way for you to show Flutter you care. What you are doing will please God AND Flutter. It's always good to look for ways to help others.*

PUPPET 2: *We learned at church that Elisha, in the Bible, showed that he cared for the poor widow by helping her.*

PONDER: *So we decided to be like Elisha and help Flutter.*

LEADER: *That's a very kind thing to do! Do you need some help? I'd like to help too.*

**PONDER &
PUPPET 2:** *Sure! Here's a brush.* (One puppet hands a brush to Leader, and they all paint for a few moments before ending.)

GP49: Different Jobs for Different Folks

Cast: Ponder the Frog, Noah's Park Puppet #2

Puppet 2 is onstage, sleeping.

PONDER: *(Calling name of Puppet 2.)* **Wake up! Wake up! I need some help!** *(Shakes Puppet 2.)* **Come on, there's work to do.**

PUPPET 2: *(Wakes up suddenly.)* **Huh? What? Oh, Ponder, I was dreaming. It was a terrible dream. I'm glad you woke me.**

PONDER: **Well, you can tell me about it as we walk to Cozy Cave. We need to go there to clean it up. In fact, the whole park has gotten messy!**

PUPPET 2: **You know, Ponder. I've noticed that. Look at all the trash lying around. And look at all the things that haven't been put away or straightened up.**

PONDER: **It seems like no one is helping to keep things tidy anymore. We have to figure out a way solve this problem.**

PUPPET 2: **That's odd. In my dream, I was all alone in Noah's Park. There was trash everywhere. No one was helping to keep things tidy. I was working all by myself to clean it up, but there was so much to do. I kept thinking,**

"*Where is everybody? Why aren't they helping me?*" (*Shakes head.*) **I didn't like THAT dream!**

PONDER: *Your dream is more real than you think. Noah's Park needs to be cleaned up!*

PUPPET 2: *But Noah's Park is so big. How will we get it all done?*

PONDER: *I have an idea! Let's have a Noah's Park cleanup meeting. All the animals should come. We can talk about how EVERYONE needs to help a little. Each animal could do a different job.*

PUPPET 2: *Yeah! The tall animals and the ones that can climb could straighten up the treetops. The smallest animals could straighten up the ground.*

PONDER: *And the animals that swim—like me— could clean up the pond.*

PUPPET 2: *That's a great idea, Ponder! I think God showed you a good way for all of us to care for Noah's Park and each other! I'm glad God gave you the job of being in charge of us.*

PONDER: *God gives each of us a different job. And each of our jobs is important.*

PUPPET 2: *Let's start calling all the animals. We have a lot to do!* (*Exit.*)

GP50: Hide and Seek a Nap

Cast: Noah's Park Puppet #2, and Ponder, the Frog.

Props: A large rock, placed near the side of the stage

Puppet 2 looks around frantically.

PUPPET 2: *Oh! Where can I hide? I don't want Shadow to find me!*

PONDER: *(Enters.)* **Hello,** *(Name of puppet.)***! What are you doing?**

PUPPET 2: *(Yells in surprise.)* **Aaah! Oh, Ponder! You scared me! I'm looking for a hiding place where NObody can find me.**

PONDER: **Well, how about over there—behind that rock?** *(Points to the rock.)*

PUPPET 2: **Yes! That's it! The rock is a great idea, Ponder.** *(Partially hides behind the rock.)* **How's this? Can you still see me?**

PONDER: **Just a little. Say,** *(Name of puppet.)***, why are you hiding?**

PUPPET 2: **I want to take my nap, Ponder. But Shadow wants me to play with him, so I'm hiding. I like playing with Shadow, but if I miss my nap, I'll feel tired and cranky later. Besides, I LIKE napping. Doesn't Shadow care?**

PONDER: **I think Shadow would care if he**

knew. But I know someone who knows AND cares about you.

PUPPET 2: (Peeking further out) **Who is that, Ponder?**

PONDER: **I'm talking about Jesus! Jesus knows where you are, no matter where you are hiding. He knows all about you. And Jesus knows you need your nap. And better yet, Jesus really cares about you.**

PUPPET 2: (Coming out from hiding.) **Wow! Do you mean that Jesus knows where I am right now? He knows I need my nap?**

PONDER: **Yes! He knows—and He cares.**

PUPPET 2: (Listening to noises offstage.) **Uh-oh! Ponder, I have to run and hide now. I think I hear Shadow coming. Maybe Jesus will help me hide. I DO need a nap, you know.** (He yawns noisily.) **See you later.** (Exits.)

GP51: Love Those Neighbors!

Cast: Ponder the Frog, Noah's Park Puppet #2

Ponder is onstage.

PUPPET 2: *(Enters, calling to someone offstage.)* **I don't care! I don't want them coming into Noah's Park!** *(Nearly walks into Ponder.)*

PONDER: **Excuse me,** *(Name of Puppet 2.)*. **Am I interrupting something?**

PUPPET 2: **Oh, no, Ponder. I am quite finished! I was just talking to a friend. Or someone who USED to be a friend. He wants to invite that new family of apes to Cozy Cave for a "Welcome to the Neighborhood Party." I told him no way! Imagine that! Apes! In Noah's Park!**

PONDER: **What's so bad about that?**

PUPPET 2: **You've got to be kidding, Ponder! Don't you know? Apes are VERY dirty animals. I have heard that they NEVER take a bath. AND they don't like to share. We in Noah's Park don't WANT that kind of neighbor.**

PONDER: **I'm surprised at you,** *(Name of puppet.)*. **You are acting very unkindly. Do you know this family?**

PUPPET 2: **Well, no. Not yet anyway. I suppose I'll get to know them soon enough.**

PONDER: *I think your friend has a good idea.*

PUPPET 2: *You do?*

PONDER: *Yes! We SHOULD welcome them to Noah's Park. The Bible says that we are to show love to our neighbors. What better way to do that than by having a welcome party for them?*

PUPPET 2: *But, Ponder. You don't understand. They're DIFFERENT from us!*

PONDER: *I know. And YOU and I are different too. Yet we are friends. Right?*

PUPPET 2: *Yes, but . . .*

PONDER: *Now, now. If we are going to obey God, we should show our neighbors that we love them. Just because they look different from us or act different, that's no reason to be unkind to them.*

PUPPET 2: *(Hangs his head.) Ponder, I think you're right. I'm sorry.*

PONDER: *Well, I think we can all be wrong sometimes. (Name of puppet.), I think if you get to know this family, you might even begin to like them. I've heard some really nice things about them.*

PUPPET 2: *Really? I think I'll try God's way. I'm going to go find my friend and tell him I'll help with the party.*

PONDER: *Great! Tell him I'd like to help too! (Both exit.)*

GP52: Thanks!

Cast: Ponder, Noah's Park Puppet #2, a Leader

Props: A small comb

Ponder and Leader are chatting when Noah's Park Puppet #2 interrupts.

PONDER: *. . . And that's when I said . . .*

PUPPET 2: *(Runs onstage, interrupts excitedly.) Oh, what will I do?! Hey, Ponder! Hey, (Name of Leader.)! My fur is all matted and I can't find my comb! My mom said I have to get it combed right away before our visitors get here! What will I do?*

LEADER: *I have a comb you can borrow. (Holds up comb.) Would you like it?*

PUPPET 2: *(Grabs the comb and runs offstage yelling.) A comb! I found it! I have a comb!*

(Leader and Ponder look at each other, wondering what to say.)

LEADER: *Um, well, that was interesting.*

PONDER: *Quite honestly, I thought our little animal friend would at least say thank you.*

LEADER: *Well, I kind of expected that too. But there seemed to be a big rush, and a comb is just a little thing. So, I guess I understand.*

PONDER: *But wouldn't it be so much more pleasant if everyone would just remember to say thank you? You know, this reminds me of a Bible story. I remember how Jesus helped so MANY people. But not everyone bothered to thank Him.*

LEADER: *I can think of several stories when people thanked Jesus—or they DIDN'T. But you know, sometimes I do it too.*

PONDER: *What's that?*

LEADER: *I forget to say thank you to Jesus. He does so MANY things for me. He answers so MANY prayers. He helps me in so MANY ways. I often don't take the time to really thank Him. And I should.*

PONDER: *Yes, we all should.*

LEADER: *I think I'm going to put that on my list of things to do each night at bed-time.* (Pretends to think of his list.) **Let's see, brush teeth, put on pajamas, hug Mom and Dad, and . . . thank Jesus— for MANY things!**

PUPPET 2: (Rushing back in.) **Oh, I forgot! I forgot! Thank you,** (Name of leader.)**! Thank you!** (Turns around and rushes back offstage.)

(Leader and Ponder look at each other in amazement, then exit laughing.)

GP53: Lonely Days

Cast: Ponder the Frog, Noah's Park Puppet #2

PUPPET 2: *(Sighing.)* **Boy, I wish someone would come and play with me. I think no one likes me anymore.** *(He brightens up as Ponder enters.)* **Hi, Ponder! Do you want to play with me?**

PONDER: **Hello,** *(Name of puppet.).* **No, I'm sorry I can't play right now. I'm on my way to visit Flutter, the Dove. She just got home from her trip south. She has some news to share with me.**

PUPPET 2: *(Moaning pitifully.)* **Oh, no! Not YOU too! Nobody likes me! No one wants to play with me today. I feel so lonely!**

PONDER: **Well, now! What's the matter with you,** *(Name of puppet.)***? You're usually a very cheerful animal.**

PUPPET 2: **Everyone is too busy to play with me today—even my best friend. I feel so lonely. What can I do, Ponder? I don't like being sad.**

PONDER: *(Looks up at ceiling and speaks aloud to himself.)* **Hmmm. Let me see. I wonder what Noah would say to him?** *(Looks at Puppet 2.)* *(Name of puppet.),* **you've been learning at church how much Jesus cares for each one of us.**

PUPPET 2: *That's right, Ponder, I have. But what does that have to do with being lonely?*

PONDER: *Jesus not only cares about you, He also KNOWS all about you. He knows when you feel sad or lonely. And you also need to remember that Jesus is always with you. He's our "forever Friend."*

PUPPET 2: *You know, Ponder, if Jesus KNOWS about me and CARES about me and is always WITH me, then I don't have to feel so lonely. I could just talk to Him anytime—right now, even! And then I wouldn't be so lonely, right?*

PONDER: *Right!*

PUPPET 2: *And I think Jesus sent you to me today just to cheer me up. Say, Ponder, after you visit Flutter, would you play with me then?*

PONDER: *Sure, (Name of puppet.). I'll see you later. (Exit.)*